To: _____

From: _____

SIMPLE ACTS

Other books by Gregory E. Lang:

Life Maps

Love Signs

Why a Daughter Needs a Dad

Why a Son Needs a Dad

Why I Love Grandma

Why I Love Grandpa

Why a Son Needs a Mom

Why a Daughter Needs a Mom

Why I Chose You

Why I Love You

Why I Need You

Why We Are a Family

Brothers and Sisters

Why We Are Friends

SIMPLE

CREATING HAPPINESS FOR
YOURSELF & THOSE YOU LOVE

ACTS

GREGORY E. LANG

CUMBERLAND HOUSE
NASHVILLE, TENNESSEE

SIMPLE ACTS
PUBLISHED BY CUMBERLAND HOUSE PUBLISHING, INC.
431 Harding Industrial Drive
Nashville, TN 37211

Cover design: James Duncan Creative, Nashville, TN
Text design: Lisa Taylor
Photographs: Gregory E. Lang

ISBN-13: 978-1-58182-566-4
ISBN-10: 1-58182-566-8

Printed in the United States of America
1 2 3 4 5 6 7 — 11 10 09 08 07 06

To Jill, Meagan, and Linley—my family, my greatest source of happiness.

Introduction

✳ WHAT IS HAPPINESS? The temporary joy you feel when something good happens? The state of contentment you find yourself in when everything in your life is going well? Is it a spiritual state of well-being? Or the pleasure that comes from making someone else happy? Is it all of these? No matter how you define happiness, it is something we all want and seek.

I am deliriously happy, but I haven't always been. There was a time in my life when I misunderstood happiness, when I thought it was complex and elusive, and not meant for me. I didn't learn until later, but thankfully not too late, that happiness is actually quite simple and, indeed, meant for everyone. I learned that happiness can come from so many simple, seemingly inconsequential things, most of which can be done anywhere at any time, with little effort, and yet can yield a significant, and sometimes lasting, effect.

That is what this book is about—those simple acts you can do to increase your happiness and make others happy as well. It isn't too profound, too intellectual, or too esoteric; it's just a collection of thoughts and suggestions, some silly, some sweet, some more creative than others, that are sure to make you and others laugh and smile, again and again. Who isn't happy after a good laugh?

Do you need a book to find happiness? you might ask. Well, if you are looking for happiness, then yes, you do need this book. Because it will help you understand that happiness isn't found, it is *made*. You see, happiness isn't external to you, something you can buy or earn—it is something within you. All of us have the ability to create our own happiness; we just need to find our personal outlet for its expression. The simple acts described in the following pages are meant to help you find your outlet. Try a few—heck, maybe even all of them. You'll soon see that laughter and happiness follow when you act in simple, unexpected, gracious, or humorous ways.

Once you've learned how to create your own happiness and are having fun doing it, take steps to attend to the spirit of others, especially those you love. Let your quest for happiness become about creating it for someone else rather than yourself. Realizing that you have the power to bring smiles of joy to those you care about, when you see that something you've done makes another happy, is when you become *really* happy!

So go out and have some fun, and do something for someone else in the process. Not only will you put a smile on their face, you'll end up with one on yours too—I promise.

SIMPLE
ACTS

I. Find animals in the clouds.

2. Don't be afraid of having a meaningful connection with someone you just met.

3. Remember a sweet goodbye that left you knowing someone cared about you? Give one to someone else.

4. See if you can finish an important project *before* the deadline.

5. Call your best friend and chat for a while.

6. Watch for smiles from passing strangers. Be sure to smile back.

7. Look through your high school yearbook; it is full of good memories. Draw a mustache on an old nemesis.

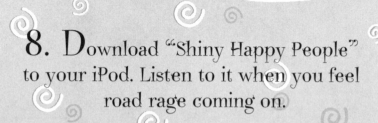

8. Download "Shiny Happy People" to your iPod. Listen to it when you feel road rage coming on.

9. Have a slumber party with a few close friends.

10. Jump on the bed. Watch out for the ceiling fan!

11. Read a page a day from a bathroom humor book.

12. Learn how to make at least
one origami figure.

13. Have a picnic in the park.

14. Write a silly poem about someone you
know and then share it with that person.

15. Tell a joke to a stranger
and then ask them to tell you one.

16. Find a place where you can go
occasionally for peace and quiet.

17. End your day with a prayer.

18. Believe in angels. Be one.

19. Come to understand why you did
something you now regret. Learn from it.
Don't do it again.

20. Prove to someone that no matter what, you are a true friend.

21. Offer someone three wishes and then do all you can to make them come true.

22. Remember your childhood heroes. Bring one up somehow in your next conversation.

23. Be passionate with someone you love.

24. Come in from the cold and warm your buns against a fireplace.

25. Catch snowflakes on your tongue.

26. Offer someone sweet whispers of affection.

27. Start a snowball or water balloon fight with your neighbors.

28. Splash around in a mud puddle.

29. Take a lazy fishing trip.

30. Play a board game with a child.

31. Make gingerbread man cookies—
really big ones.

32. Decorate a Christmas tree with
homemade ornaments.

33. Wrap a gift for someone special;
put several boxes inside one another.

34. Imagine what the next day could bring. Make it happen.

35. Have a habit of looking forward, not backward.

36. Go to a wedding; be sure to kiss the bride.

37. Plan a surprise party for someone.

38. Try your best at everything you do.

39. Do something to change someone's life.

40. When you think something about you has changed for the better, call and give credit to the person who most inspired the change.

41. Ask a teenager to teach you something you don't know how to do.

42. Give a child a stuffed animal.

43. Tell a child he or she can read your mind. No matter what they "read," tell them they are correct.

44. Connect someone's freckles and have them connect yours.

45. Go to a fair and eat a funnel cake.

46. Wear a fake mustache to work one day.

47. Attend a high school ball game.
Eat a hotdog. Yell a lot.

48. Start a benign rumor about yourself, then
wait and see what the story becomes
by the time it makes its way back to you.

49. Stand in the front yard and yodel.

50. Celebrate your pet's birthday.

51. During a tension-filled scene at a scary movie, yell out, "Behind you!"

52. Use the word *doody* in a conversation with your boss.

53. Put spinning hubcaps on your mother's car.

54. Tape toilet paper to your shoe and then walk through the mall.

55. On your next visit to a seafood restaurant, ask if they serve jellyfish.

56. Invent a new ice cream flavor and submit it to Ben & Jerry's.

57. Write down your plan for the future and read it in five years. It'll crack you up.

58. Buy a pair of new shoes, preferably on sale.

59. Jump as high as you can on a trampoline.

60. Jump into a pool on a hot day.

61. Test drive a sports car, preferably a red convertible.

62. Practice jumping until you can nail a slam dunk.

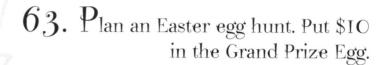

63. Plan an Easter egg hunt. Put $10 in the Grand Prize Egg.

64. Sing along with "The Star-Spangled Banner" at all ball games.

65. Stay in your pajamas all day long.

66. Send a Valentine's Day card
to someone who least expects to get one.

67. Make a surprise phone call to catch up
with someone who was once important to you.

68. Remember the butterflies
in your stomach when you first fell in love?
Do something to recreate that sensation.

69. Close your eyes and visualize your first
kiss. If you still know that person, kiss 'em again.

70. Have a really romantic tussle with your mate.

71. Ask for a gentle touch from a loved one. Reciprocate it.

72. Make a wall mural from pictures of your loved ones.

73. Do something that will bring tears of joy to someone you love.

74. Blow bubbles. Try to make a really big one.

75. Put some peanut butter on the roof of your dog's mouth, but not too much.

76. Start a sing-along in the car. Keep singing until everyone joins in.

77. Start a wave at a ball game.

78. Sport a temporary tattoo in a not-so-well-hidden place.

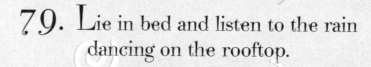

79. Lie in bed and listen to the rain dancing on the rooftop.

80. Remember a special moment you wished would never end? Close your eyes and relive it.

81. Watch a Hallmark commercial on television. Don't be afraid to cry.

82. Stay out later than usual one night. Spend this time with someone who needs to talk.

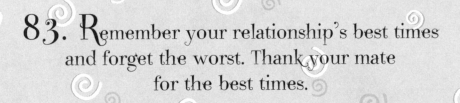

83. Remember your relationship's best times and forget the worst. Thank your mate for the best times.

84. Open a savings account for someone and keep it a secret until a very rainy day comes along.

85. Say the words that you know will touch someone's heart. Make sure they hear you.

86. Name your big dogs "Tinkerbelle" and "Sweetie Pie" and your little ones "Thor" and "Zeus."

87. Memorize a few silly quotes by famous people. Throw one out now and then.

88. Choose an outrageous story from a tabloid newspaper and see if you can make others believe it is true.

89. Have your caricature portrait drawn
and put it on display at your office.

90. Always wear a crown or tiara
on your birthday.

91. Make a photo album with pictures
of your favorite funny moments. Leave it
on your coffee table for others to enjoy.

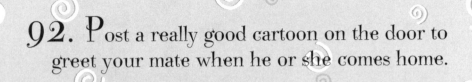

92. Post a really good cartoon on the door to greet your mate when he or she comes home.

93. Wait outside for someone's arrival. Jump up and down when they get out of the car.

94. Admit to and laugh at your weird habits.

95. Ask someone to look in your eyes and tell you what they see. Disagree and ask them to look again.

96. Overlook an imperfection in someone who values your opinion and acceptance.

97. Admit to a time when you were wrong.

98. Learn something new each day. It keeps the brain sharp.

99. Call your dad and tell him thanks for all he has done for you.

IOO. Set an achievable goal and keep track of your progress. Reward yourself when you get there.

IOI. Get something off your chest, but do it tactfully.

IO2. Prove to yourself that you can control your emotions.

IO3. Make someone proud of you.

104. Drink hot cocoa with marshmallows on cold weekend afternoons.

105. Eat a homemade oatmeal-raisin cookie just out of the oven.

106. Lie in the grass and take a nap.

107. Have guests over during the holidays.

108. Clean house to your favorite music. It makes the job go faster.

109. Allow yourself to take a power nap every now and then.

110. Commit an anonymous act of kindness.

111. Cuddle with a newborn.

112. Listen to favorite songs from your past.

113. Pause and look into the smiling face of a child.

114. Hug your teammates, whether you've won or lost.

115. Help someone understand an inside joke.

Marriages are made in heaven and consummated on Earth.

Be charitable, it will be appreciated

116. Keep a jar of fortune cookies close at hand. Have one when you feel blue. Where else can you get a pick-me-up and dessert at the same time?

117. Give someone a coupon redeemable for one hour of your time. Let them "cash it in" whenever they need to.

118. Sit on the porch and read the paper in the warmth of the morning sun.

119. Tie messages of hope and good cheer to balloons and release them over the neighborhood.

120. Give someone butterfly kisses.

121. Listen to the birds sing their morning songs.

122. Leave an uplifting letter where a stranger will find it.

123. Decide *not* to get a face-lift, and then tell everyone you just saved $10,000.

124. Crash a homecoming dance.

125. Send a surprise e-mail to an old friend.

126. Write down the name of every person you kissed in high school, in chronological order. Who was the best?

127. Overstate your income and understate your age the next time you fill out a warranty card.

128. Try talking under water.

129. Take a road trip with the windows down and the radio cranked up.

130. Play Scrabble with yourself, and play to win.

131. Eat a piece of chocolate peanut butter fudge. Maybe two pieces.

132. Make up words from the letters floating in your alphabet soup.

133. Start a long conversation about a subject that really matters to someone else.

134. Let someone you respect know you do and why.

135. Realize that someone out there wants to be just like you.

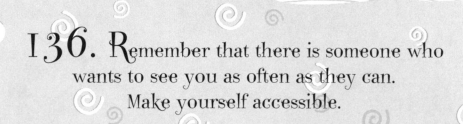

136. Remember that there is someone who wants to see you as often as they can. Make yourself accessible.

137. Attend a school play or band concert. Be the last to stop applauding.

138. Ask an older adult to tell you about how things used to be.

139. Take one of Mom's secret recipes and make it for her as a surprise.

140. Put a little extra whipped cream on your next slice of pie.

141. Watch fireworks on the Fourth of July.

142. Read a bedtime story to a child.

143. Pretend to be a child again— play hard, very hard.

144. Watch an old episode of *The Little Rascals*.

145. Hang your head out the car window
and enjoy the fresh air.

146. Sit in a cool breeze
on a hot summer day.

147. Read a favorite book once more.

148. Tell everyone how you used to be the lead singer for a punk band called "Quasimodo and the Bell Tones."

149. Own at least one pair of really funky shoes—and then have the nerve to wear them!

150. Have an Opposite Day.

151. Hide in a cardboard box.

152. On your way to your next meeting, tango down the hall.

153. Have a crush on a celebrity. Send a fan letter.

154. Go bowling, even if you don't play well. Cheer for all your gutter balls.

155. Invite your neighbor over for dinner and then act surprised when they show up.

156. Tickle someone.

157. Let someone tickle you.

158. Buy a new coffee mug, one with a funny cartoon on it.

159. Get one of those magnet business signs made for your car and dream up a fun, outrageous business name, like "Mobile Psychic" or "Squirrel Whisperer."

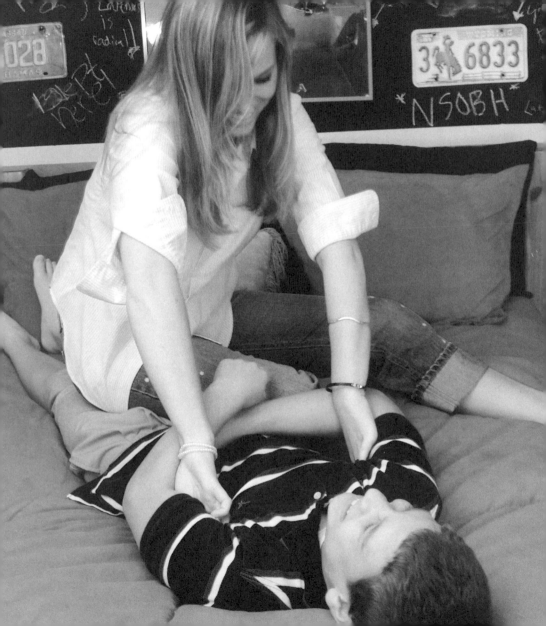

160. Cross the finish line in every race.

161. Say "thank you" for the kindness
of a stranger.

162. Play a card game with friends.
You pick the game.

163. Tell someone about your faith.

164. When you need a friend, call someone who will ask, "How are you?" with sincerity.

165. Get dressed up for a party. Wear your finest. It's better to be overdressed than underdressed.

166. Frame one of your child's artwork pieces and hang it in the house for all to see.

167. Plan a cookout with friends.

168. Open a Christmas present early.

169. Build the wackiest snowman you can imagine.

170. Go to Grandma's house and eat all her cookies.

171. Watch little children at play.

172. Listen to the sounds of the ocean with your eyes closed. Let the rhythm of the waves lull you to sleep.

173. Take a day off work and go shopping or to a matinee.

174. Act carefree and unashamed at least once a day.

175. Get a kiss or hug at least once a day.

176. Go dancing and dance like a fool. Stay late enough to close the place down.

177. Ask a cashier if they take common sense.

178. Laugh at your own stupidity.

179. See how many Whoppers you can get in your mouth at once, but be careful.

180. Mount a bobble head doll to the hood of your car.

181. When asked what you're thinking, answer, "If *W* is one letter, why is it pronounced with two (or is it three) syllables?"

182. Wear some of those redneck Bubba teeth to your next dental appointment.

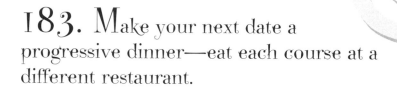

183. Make your next date a progressive dinner—eat each course at a different restaurant.

184. Have some chocolate-chip ice cream in a just-baked waffle cone.

185. Mix a little Tabasco sauce with your ketchup.

186. Eat breakfast for dinner.
Be sure to have a mimosa.

187. Float in a pool, favorite beverage in hand.

188. Order a pizza with
all your favorite toppings.

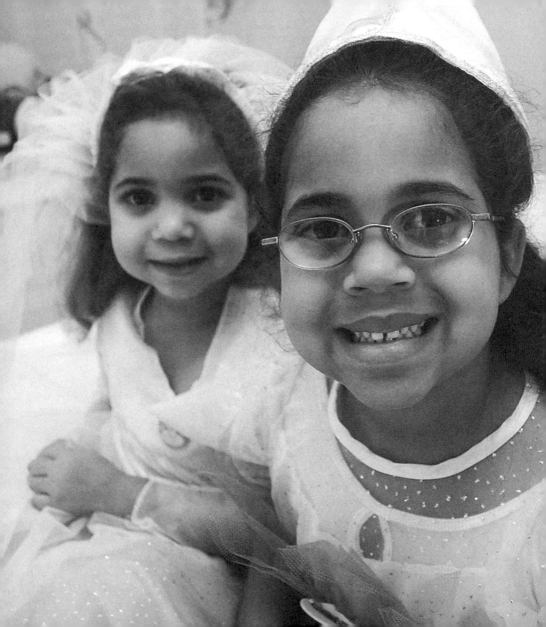

189. No matter your age, wear a new costume every Halloween.

190. Paint a room a new color.

191. Make a collage from old photographs for your desk.

192. Play hide-and-seek. You're never too old for it.

193. Play an April Fools' joke on someone you know will take it well.

194. Listen to Christmas music any time of the year.

195. The next time someone asks why you moved, tell them it was the idea of the witness protection program.

196. Go out for some fresh-baked doughnuts and a hot cup of coffee.

197. Make margarita popsicles.

198. Sing along with the early Beatles' hits.

199. Buy a Dilbert calendar.

200. Take a family photograph,
but before giving it to others, use photo editing
software to remove everyone's hair.

201. Buy a pair of cheap, funky sunglasses and claim they once belonged to Elton John.

202. When on a plane, ask your seatmate if you can have their air sick bag.

203. Buy a little doodad to help accessorize a room.

204. Go see a concert at an outdoor venue.

205. Surround yourself with friends, lots of them.

206. Go visit your parents.

207. Go the extra mile, even if you'll be the only one to know about it.

208. Flirt with a stranger, but only a little.

209. Look at your trophies, certificates, and ribbons. Pat yourself on the back.

210. Give someone another chance.

211. Tell someone, "You look great today! Really great. Hot even!"

212. Love someone with everything you've got.

213. Teach yourself how to use chopsticks.

214. Keep a box of chocolate-covered cherries in the freezer. Pop one after a bad day.

215. Draw a self-portrait and tape it to your refrigerator.

216. Hold someone's hand and say a prayer together.

217. Get personalized stationery.

218. Know that no matter what you have done, God loves you anyway.

219. Take an acting class.

220. Start reading a new book, one that's different from your usual book selections.

221. Sing loudly in church, and use your hands.

222. Throw all your pennies in a fountain and wish something great for someone else with each coin.

223. Meet a friend for lunch
at your favorite restaurant.

224. Listen to someone without once
interrupting with your own opinion or point of
view. It's very validating and will be appreciated.

225. The next time you tell someone
they did a good job, say it loud enough
for others to overhear.

226. List all the reasons that get you out of bed in the morning.

227. Go camping for the weekend. Tell ghost stories around the campfire.

228. Buy several boxes of your favorite Girl Scout cookies.

229. Watch a late-night comedy show and eat some of those Girl Scout cookies.

230. Learn an impressive card trick and perform it at parties.

231. Order your crème brûlée warm.

232. Go to where you are sure to hear laughter. Join in.

233. Walk through the neighborhood— backward.

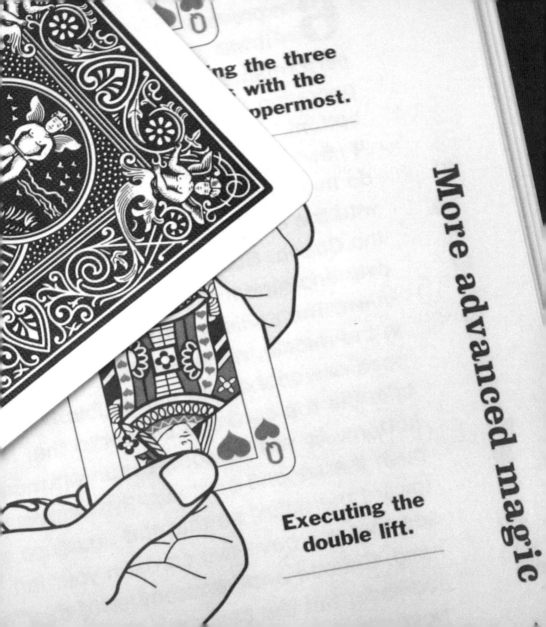

ng the three
with the
ppermost.

Executing the
double lift.

234. Write the best-darn-sweetest love letter you can think of and mail it to the one who wants most to receive it from you.

235. Allow your heart to lead you now and then.

236. Believe in yourself, not the naysayer.

237. Sing a favorite love song
to the one you love.

238. Go see a romantic movie.
Don't resist crying.

239. Tell someone something
you like about them.

240. Find yourself held in someone's arms.

241. Watch the sun set over the ocean.

242. Stand beneath a waterfall.

243. Pull over and look at a rainbow.

244. Sit outside and watch for falling stars.

245. Ask a child to tell you about her imaginary friend.

246. Teach a child how to get a trucker to use the air horn.

247. Hand out candy cigars at a party.

248. Search until you find the good in someone who irritates you.

249. Take the time to ask about your co-workers' family life.

250. Tell someone about your dreams. Ask them about theirs.

251. Read the Sunday-morning comics
in your pajamas.

252. Put too few candles
on your birthday cake.

253. Relax on a sailboat.

254. Stop taking yourself so seriously.

255. Play Simon Says with a child.

256. Lean over, right now,
and touch your toes.

257. Write a press release at your next
birthday and fax it to your hometown newspaper.
Brag a little; it's permitted on this day.

258. Eat blue cotton candy.

259. Hide a whoopee cushion
in someone's chair.

260. Bake a cake and give it a really thick
coat of icing, topped off with lots of sprinkles.

261. Put a sarcastic bumper sticker
on your car.

262. Help someone resolve a dispute.

263. Browse the self-improvement shelves and realize how fortunate you are.

264. Add something to your favorite collection.

265. Visit somewhere you have never been.

266. Join a club or organization.

267. Befriend an enemy.

268. Ask everyone in your family to get together for a worship service and have lunch together afterward.

269. Sit on Santa Claus's lap
and ask for a pony.

270. Play with a puppy or kitten.

271. Find a pastry shop
and have some baklava.

272. Remember your imaginary friends.
Strike up a conversation with one of them.
They've missed you.

273. Take a moment to look in the mirror. Tell yourself you look fantastic!

274. Laugh out loud for no reason.

275. Watch your home movies with your family.

276. Go to a party and take as many pictures as you can. Make copies for everyone and write a funny commentary on each one.

277. Overeat without guilt
at Thanksgiving dinner.

278. Start a "Co-worker of the Week" tradition at the office. Such pats on the back from peers are cheap but priceless.

279. Save a voicemail of you giving yourself words of encouragement. Listen to it whenever you need to.

280. Give someone flowers for no particular reason.

281. Go for a walk in the rain.

282. Give a stranger a New Year's Eve kiss.

283. Go to your favorite live entertainment event. Sit near the front.

284. Build a kite with a child and then take it out and see how high it will go.

285. Hang upside down on the monkey bars.

286. Rock a baby to sleep.

287. Buy an ice cream novelty from your childhood from an ice cream truck.

288. Sit up and wait for Santa Claus.

289. Listen to a baby's first words.

290. Buy lemonade from a child's lemonade stand. Tip well.

291. Read an Amelia Bedelia book.

292. Wear fuzzy bedroom slippers once in a while.

293. Make up a new word. I invented *scrumpin'*, an urban verb for *being scrumptious.*

294. Memorize at least three good jokes, and tell them often.

295. When asked about the forecast, respond with your best "weatherman" routine.

296. Make your first kiss of each weekend last at least 30 seconds.

297. Send your mate loving text messages at random times during the day.

298. Play doctor in the dark.

299. Take a shower by candlelight.

300. Learn how to say "I love you" in a different language.

301. Instead of a card, include a personal letter with every gift.

302. Stop a clerk in a department store and ask where the liposuction clinic is.

303. Go for the Mr. Spock look the next time you get your brows waxed.

304. When in a waiting room, talk back to the television.

305. Let your co-workers overhear you asking your bank if the lottery check has cleared yet.

306. Pretend to be a reporter and interview passersby. Ask questions like, "Who would you rather dine with, Kramer or Joey, and why?"

307. Write your congressman and tell him about your alien abduction.

308. Show up at the next party you attend with a body guard.

309. Learn to play a musical instrument. It may take a while, but once you play your first song, you'll be happy, even if you are off-key.

310. Take a night class in a subject that has always interested you.

311. Post a comment on a blog or bulletin board about a subject of interest to you.

312. Shake hands and say "thanks" to a police officer or fireman.

313. Pat a child on the head and say, "You are going to be famous one day."

314. Tell the next ten friends you see that you think they've lost weight.

315. Applaud servicemen whenever you see them.

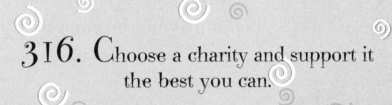

316. Choose a charity and support it the best you can.

317. When checking into a hotel, ask for an upgrade. You'll probably get it.

318. Read the notes from friends written in your high school yearbook.

319. Go to a class reunion.
It doesn't matter that it may not be your class.

320. Have an Elvis impersonator pose with you in your next family portrait.

321. Google your name and see how many times you show up on the Internet.

322. Talk back to a stand-up comedian.

323. Wear a wig once in a while.

324. Go to a card shop and read all the cards in the humor section.

325. Stop at a convenience store and tell the clerk you are on a journey of self-discovery. Ask for directions.

326. Dress your pets in seasonal costumes.

327. Make a big deal of the birthday
person at the next birthday party you attend.

328. Make silly faces at someone
acting too serious.

329. Keep a calendar of everyone's
anniversary date. Remind those who need it.

330. Inspire someone to try something new.

331. Part your hair on the opposite side and see how long it takes someone to notice.

332. Rent a canoe and paddle around a lake.

333. Build the largest sand castle you've ever seen.

334. Go to church.

335. Get a new hairstyle.

336. Go barefoot where you shouldn't.

337. Fall asleep in your favorite chair.

338. Research the meaning of your name.

339. Ride bikes with friends.

340. Visit a karaoke bar. I dare you to get up and sing.

341. Confess to your most embarrassing moment. Don't skip any of the details.

342. Ask the bank teller for a sucker.

343. While waiting in a long line, turn around and introduce yourself to the person behind you.

344. Drive around the neighborhood wearing one of those big red clown noses.

345. Use a naked baby photograph the next time you are asked to supply a head shot.

346. Order milk and a peanut butter and jelly sandwich at your next business lunch.

347. Watch an American film that has been dubbed in Japanese.

348. Have your teeth whitened.

349. Make up outrageous stories about yourself to tell at parties or on blind dates.

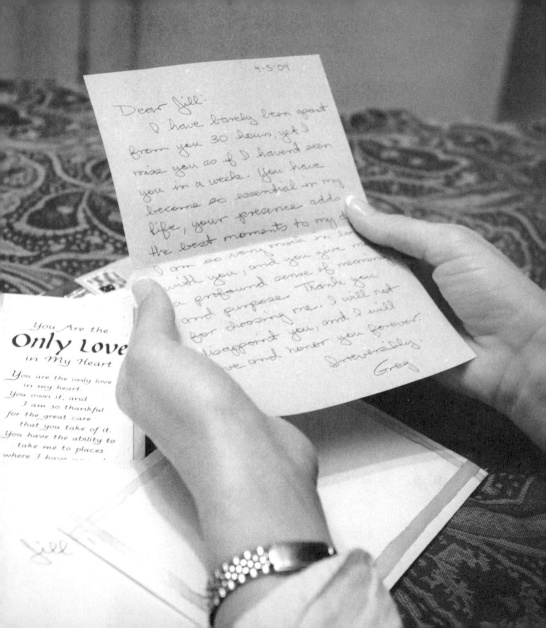

350. Sit down on a quiet afternoon and reread those old love letters and romantic cards you saved.

351. When stopped at a traffic light, smile and wave at the driver next to you.

352. Walk up to a total stranger and pay them a sincere compliment.

353. Tell all your friends you are thinking about running for president.

354. Make faces at yourself in the mirror first thing in the morning.

355. Wear a pair of those rainbow-striped toe socks with sandals.

356. Spend a day pretending you have multiple personalities.

357. Have a trademark phrase, like "Dang!"

358. Tell everyone about the time you spotted Elvis at the grocery store.

359. Offer to give someone a "Me Day," and then do anything they want to do.

360. Sit on your daddy's lap.

361. Hold your momma's hand.

362. Play peek-a-boo with an infant.

363. During the Q&A portion of the next presentation you attend, ask the speaker for his/her phone number.

364. Get to work early and write a "Good Morning" poem on the white board. Sign it with a smiley face.

365. Interject some interesting facts in your next conversation, like "There are 293 ways to make change for a dollar."

366. Call up your sibling and begin the conversation with, "Do you remember the time we. . . ."

367. Make a charitable donation in the name of someone who once helped you.

368. Visit a pet shop on adoption day and pet all the animals.

369. Eat a bowl of ice cream before you go to bed. Be liberal with the chocolate sauce.

370. Sleep on the best sheets you can afford.

371. Look to the sun with your eyes closed and let it warm your face.

372. Get a sea salt foot massage.

373. When at the beach, wiggle your toes deep into the sand.

374. Go as high as you can on a swing.

375. Climb a tree and admire nature.

376. Take a nap in a hammock.

377. Have your fortune told.

378. After an argument,
be the first to apologize.

379. Be someone's Secret Santa
every Christmas.

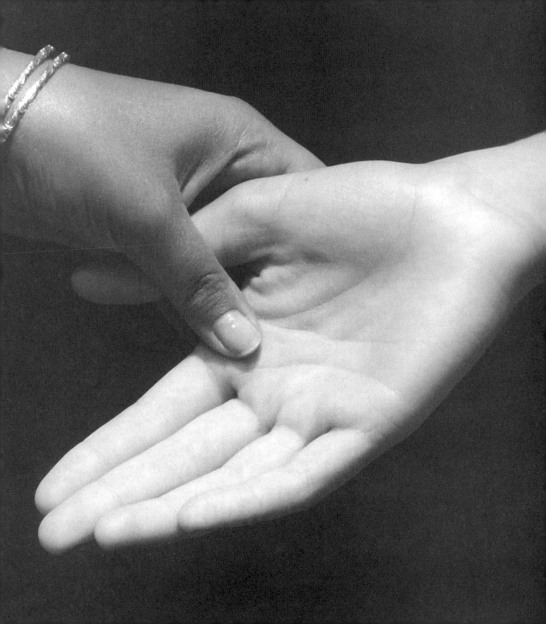

380. If in an uncomfortable situation, suggest a Happy Break. Then lead everyone in singing "If You're Happy and You Know It."

381. Walk up to a stranger and announce that they look just like someone famous.

382. Occasionally answer your phone, "Steven Spielberg."

383. Send a secret admirer note to someone.

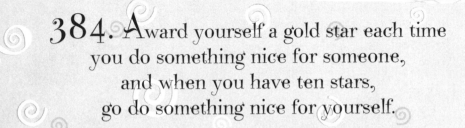

384. Award yourself a gold star each time
you do something nice for someone,
and when you have ten stars,
go do something nice for yourself.

385. Make a list of all the things you like
about yourself. Be honest, be thorough.

386. When reading to a child, use a
different and wacky voice for each character.

387. Take your in-laws out to lunch.

388. Follow all of your doctor's advice.

389. Volunteer your time to a service organization doing something you value.

390. Keep some mistletoe hanging in your house, preferably in a doorway all guests must pass through.

391. Learn how to play "Chopsticks" on the piano.

392. Learn how to say "thank you" in several different languages.

393. Stop ordering the same old thing. Experiment the next time you eat out.

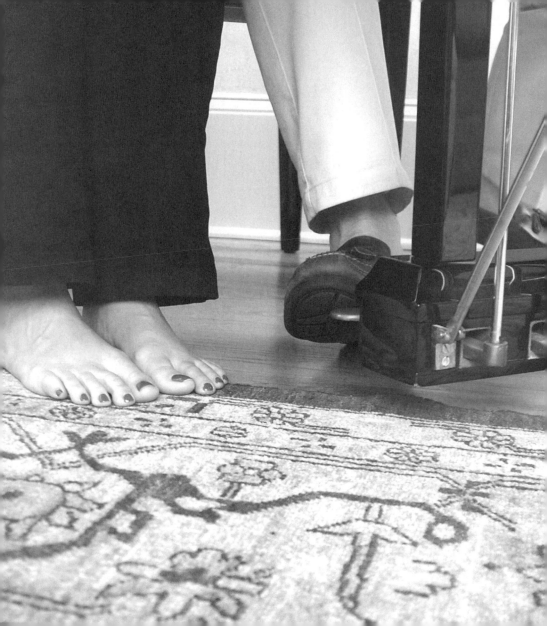

394. The next time you're at a pet store, tell the clerk you'd like to review their animal rights policy.

395. When quizzed by a nosy person, answer from the point of view of your alter ego.

396. For a day, try to end every sentence with the word *dude*.

397. Give the kids next door goofy nicknames.

398. Give the most absurd answers that come to mind the next time you are asked to participate in a market research survey.

399. Use your favorite photographs as screen savers.

400. Open a college savings account for your children.

401. Pick your kids up from school in a limousine one day.

402. Practice, practice, and practice until you can bake a perfect soufflé.

403. Every once in a while splurge, *really* splurge, on a nice bottle of wine.

404. Try for a personal best at the gym at least once a month.

405. Learn how to carve a turkey with the skill of a surgeon.

406. Go to a bakery and buy a fresh loaf of bread.

407. Every once in a while eat a bowl of your favorite cereal from childhood.

408. Go out for brunch on the first day of spring.

409. Scream at the top of the Ferris wheel.

410. Go skinny dipping.
Everybody should do it at least once.

411. Tailgate with your college chums
for home games, even if it is in your backyard.

412. Get one of those old-time saloon
photographs taken, but cross-dress.

413. Bring back a souvenir from every place you visit.

414. Memorize a few Chinese proverbs and say one when no one else seems to know what to say.

415. Plan a family vacation that includes every living generation.

416. Everyone needs at least one outrageous tropical shirt. If you don't have one, get one.

417. When at a concert, sing your favorite songs at the top of your lungs.

418. Send a letter to someone you admire and ask for a signed photograph. Show it off if you get one.

419. Use your favorite song as a ring tone on your cell phone.

420. "Accidentally" think it is someone's birthday at work and gather a crowd around to sing "Happy Birthday."

421. Pick some wildflowers
and take them home.

422. Go to a park and feed
the pigeons or ducks.

423. Be the first house on your street to get
your seasonal decorations up and the last to take
them down.

424. Put a note of thanks
in your parents' cupboard.

425. Learn all the words to the Johnny Cash song "I've Been Everywhere" and sing it at parties or whenever someone asks, "Where've you been?"

426. Smile in your driver's license and passport photos.

427. Tell everyone Dr. Phil calls you for advice.

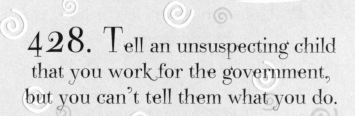

428. Tell an unsuspecting child that you work for the government, but you can't tell them what you do.

429. Why don't you and a few adult friends play Chinese Fire Drill?

430. Play rock, paper, scissors, dynamite with a kid.

431. Tell someone you want to know what it's like to walk in their shoes, and then insist they give you a pair.

432. Use room service at least once on every vacation.

433. Become a master at Spider Solitaire.

434. Finish a crossword puzzle.

435. Tape a family photo to your sun visor.

436. Memorize a Schoolhouse Rock song and hum it the next time you find yourself waiting in line. I like "Conjunction Junction."

437. Cheat on one of those free Internet IQ tests. Leave your score on screen for others to walk by and see.

438. Sleep in cartoon boxers once in a while.

439. Try to work the word *badonkadonk* into a conversation with your mother.

440. Start a blog and write a parody of yourself.

441. When in a wax museum, have a photo taken of you posed with a celebrity or dignitary. Hang the photo in your office and tell everyone how much you enjoyed meeting the person.

442. Memorize a few Groucho Marx quotes to quip at just the right moment.

443. Give yourself a rap singer nickname. Mine is Phat Poppa G.

444. Take a long walk on the beach or in the woods.

445. Sit on a dock and dangle your feet in the water.

446. Indulge yourself and fly first-class at least once.

447. Sleep late at least one Saturday morning a month.

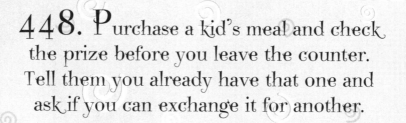

448. Purchase a kid's meal and check the prize before you leave the counter. Tell them you already have that one and ask if you can exchange it for another.

449. Have your pet photographed with Santa.

450. Give yourself enough wiggle room to hit the snooze button once in a while.

451. Add some M&Ms to your popcorn.

452. Mark all your junk mail "Return to Sender" and drop it at the post office.

453. Mock yourself in one of those family photo Christmas cards.

454. Find something absurd in the newspaper and write an over-the-top letter to the editor about it.

455. Soak yourself in a steamy bubble bath.

456. Share dessert with someone by candlelight.

457. Hang wind chimes near your kitchen window.

458. "Accidentally" reserve a room at a clothing-optional resort.

459. Hold hands with your soul mate. Don't let go.

460. Snuggle up on a sofa with someone you love.

461. Watch a classic holiday movie.

462. Make a habit of buying a card for someone every time you go where they are sold.

463. Shout out the answer the next time your pastor asks a rhetorical question during the sermon.

464. Stop at one of those photo booths and spend a few dollars. Keep some for yourself and send a few to friends.

465. As you exit the plane, ask for a pair of wings.

466. The next time someone asks you a difficult question, assume *The Thinker* position.

467. Ask the manager of a fast-food restaurant why they don't offer slow-cooked foods.

468. Pretend you have the formula for Pixie Dust.

469. Invent your own Festivus.

470. Watch your favorite *Seinfeld* episodes on a glum day. It will cheer you up.

471. End every visit with a loved one with either "I love you" or "I can't wait to see you again."

472. Ask your parents to share one of their favorite memories of your childhood.

473. Carry your most embarrassing grade-school photo in your wallet. Look at it whenever you are feeling full of yourself.

474. Invite a co-worker you don't know that well to lunch.

475. Try to shake the hand of twenty-five different people in one day.

476. Make a "Thank You" sign to keep in your car. Hold it up for someone now and then.

477. Update your Baby Book. Maybe even start a Teenager or Adult Book.

478. Add some peanuts to your soda.

479. Sprinkle a few dried cherries
on your cereal.

480. Race a few laps around the track
in a go-cart.

481. Ride a roller coaster with your hands up
the whole time.

482. Dye your hair in a crazy, but temporary, color for the weekend.

483. Make creative use of body paint.

484. Hopscotch across a parking lot in broad daylight.

485. Always test those massage chairs you see at the mall.

486. Kiss and make up with someone after a fight.

487. Get a manicure and have a little design painted on your pinkies.

488. Visit the zoo and feed the animals.

489. Read your horoscope one day and try to make it come true.

490. When purchasing a gift book for someone special, always get one written by Gregory E. Lang. Everyone will be happy.

491. Learn a new phrase, like *platitudinous ponderosity*, and use it in a conversation.

492. Spend an extra few minutes in the shower.

493. Make a name badge that identifies you as a World Peace Negotiator. Wear it often.

494. When in Vegas, use an alias.

495. Have a piñata at your birthday party. Fill it with age-appropriate treats.

496. When on a diet, reward yourself with a treat after every five pounds you lose.

497. Kiss a few frogs. You never know what could happen.

498. Write yourself an inspirational message and keep it nearby—just in case.

499. Believe in your power to be happy and never depend on someone else to make you happy.

500. Make as many people happy as you can in your lifetime.

Acknowledgments

Once more I owe a heartfelt thanks to Ron Pitkin, my publisher, who continues to have faith in the things I want to write about, and the staff at Cumberland House, most notably my editor, Lisa Taylor, a trusted resource. I also thank my wonderful wife, Jill, for her unwavering support and belief in me, and our girls, Meagan and Linley, who keep me laughing.

TO CONTACT THE AUTHOR

write in care of the publisher:
Cumberland House Publishing
431 Harding Industrial Drive
Nashville, TN 37211

or e-mail:
greg.lang@mindspring.com

visit the author's Web site:
www.gregoryelang.com